For my parents and sister who taught me the value of being nice.
–M.W.

STERLING CHILDREN'S BOOKS
New York

An Imprint of Sterling Publishing
1166 Avenue of the Americas
New York, NY 10036

ISBN 978-1-4549-1748-9

Distributed in Canada by Sterling Publishing
c/o Canadian Manda Group, 664 Annette Street
Toronto, Ontario, Canada M6S 2C8
Distributed in the United Kingdom by GMC Distribution Services
Castle Place, 166 High Street, Lewes, East Sussex, England BN7 1XU
Distributed in Australia by Capricorn Link (Australia) Pty. Ltd.
P.O. Box 704, Windsor, NSW 2756, Australia

For information about custom editions, special sales, and premium and corporate purchases,
please contact Sterling Special Sales at 800-805-5489 or specialsales@sterlingpublishing.com.

Design by Andrea Miller

Manufactured in China
Lot #:
2 4 6 8 10 9 7 5 3 1
03/16

www.sterlingpublishing.com

PLEASE BE NICE TO
SHARKS

Fascinating Facts about the Ocean's Most Misunderstood Creatures

by Matt Weiss

photos by **Matt Weiss & Daniel Botelho**

STERLING CHILDREN'S BOOKS

New York

Sharks are perhaps the most misunderstood animals in the world. Many people look at them as monsters who love to eat humans. But this isn't true! More people are injured every year from vending machines falling on them than from shark bites. Scientists estimate that humans kill over 100 million sharks each year. That's almost 200 sharks per minute. But only about five people are killed by sharks each year. The attacks that do happen are usually just misunderstandings. Humans aren't really on the menu for sharks.

Unfortunately, sharks are ending up on our dinner tables. They are hunted by humans for both their fins and for sport. Shark fin soup is a Chinese delicacy, and 70 million sharks are killed every year for this food. As a result, sharks are disappearing at an alarming rate. Some scientists estimate that certain populations have declined by 99 percent! That's right—almost all the sharks in the ocean are gone! If we keep hunting sharks, they will become extinct, and that's a real tragedy.

Losing sharks would be disastrous for both the ocean and for people. Even though humans live on land, the ocean is hugely important to us. It covers almost three-quarters of Earth's surface and contains between 50 to 80 percent of all life on the planet. There are between 700,000 and one million plant and animal species in the ocean, some of which we rely on for food. Sharks are a keystone species, which means they keep ocean animal populations in check. The food web is a complex, delicate thing. Without sharks, that web would collapse and most of the oceans would be changed forever. So, sharks are kind of the caretakers of the ocean. And they have been doing a great job of it for over 450 million years! Please, be nice to sharks! That way, they can continue to help keep our planet healthy.

WHALE SHARK

Greetings, landlubber! I'm a **whale shark**, the largest fish in the world. I weigh almost 30 tons (about 27 metric tons) on average and can grow over 40 feet (12 meters) long. That's bigger than your school bus! But don't go like a hiding clam—I eat only tiny fish and plankton. I don't even have teeth! I'm a filter feeder, so I don't need teeth to chew my food. You wouldn't pick on a guy with no teeth, would you? Be nice to me! Be nice to whale sharks!

Hey, you! You ever see a fish that walks? Well, I do . . . kind of. I'm a **bamboo shark,** one of the smallest sharks. But I can show you a cool trick. I bend my body from side to side and hop around coral reefs looking for tiny fish to eat. In fact, I only swim when I feel threatened. I also have barbels near my nostrils. These whisker-like sensors help me find food buried in the sand. It makes me look like I have a pretty sweet mustache. Don't you wish you had an awesome mustache that helped you find chocolate cake or whatever you humans eat? Speaking of humans and food, my mouth is so small, I could never eat anything as big as a human. So please be nice to bamboo sharks!

HAMMERHEAD SHARK

What's up? I'm a **scalloped hammerhead shark.** I'm named for my funky-shaped head that also gives me incredible 360-degree vision to find my food. I'm a party animal, and I love hanging out with my other shark friends. We swim in huge packs called schools, which can sometimes get as big as 500 members. But even though we love to party, we get pretty scared of humans. We love midnight snacks and do most of our eating after dark. But it's not all fun and games for us. We are "globally endangered," because 95 percent of us have been fished out of the ocean. Humans hunt us just to make us into soup! Please be nice to scalloped hammerhead sharks and party on!

TIGER SHARK

Oh, hello there! I'm a **tiger shark**. Don't get confused by my name—I'm not actually a tiger. When tiger sharks are young, our skin has a stripe pattern that makes us look tiger-like. Confusing, huh? While we're talking about sharkskin, I should mention that our skin isn't like that of most fish. It's covered in tiny V-shaped scales that are actually a lot more like teeth than scales! This helps us swim faster and smoother through the vast ocean. In fact, Olympic swimmers have worn swimsuits that perfectly mimic sharkskin so that they can swim faster. See, we're helping you out! Please, be nice to tiger sharks!

SHORTFIN MAKO SHARK

Hey, pal, I'm a **shortfin mako shark**, but my friends call me "blue dynamite." Why, you ask? 'Cause look at me—I'm a good-looking fish! Not only that, but I'm fast. Like really fast. I can swim up to 50 miles (80.5 kilometers) per hour, as fast as a lion can run! I am a speedster, but I'm also pretty smart. Some scientists say I have the largest brain-to-body ratio of any shark. The fastest and smartest—not too shabby, huh? So, please be nice to mako sharks!

BLUE SHARK

Ahoy, matey! I'm a **blue shark**. I'm pretty easy to recognize because I've got a big ol' nose and nice blue skin. Want to know else something pretty unique about blue sharks? We are masters of teamwork. That's right—when we go hunting, we hunt in a group. It's more fun to dine with friends anyway, right? But humans are never on our menu. Since the year 1580, only thirteen humans have been bitten by blue sharks. Only four of those humans died. But ten to twenty MILLION blue sharks are fished each year! So, please be nice to blue sharks!

GREAT WHITE SHARK

Hi, friend! I'm a **great white shark**, and I'm not as mean as people think. Look, I'm even smiling for this nice photographer! I'm one of the oldest animals in the world, and I've been doing my thing in the ocean for millions of years. Most of the time, I'm just peacefully roaming the seas. However, humans don't seem to like my kind much, and they have hunted a lot of my friends. Now, some scientists think that there are fewer great white sharks than there are pandas in the wild. So, please be nice to great white sharks—there are only a few of us left!

GREAT WHITE SHARK FACTS

- **Length:** Around 11 to 13 feet (3.5 to 4 meters), but can be up to 21 feet (6.5 meters).
- **Weight:** Around 1,500 to 2,400 pounds (650 to 1,100 kilograms)—the largest predatory fish in the world!
- **Speed:** Up to 25 miles (40 kilometers) per hour!
- **Diet:** Large fish, seals, sea lions, and even other sharks sometimes.
- **Life-span:** Up to 70 years.
- **Location:** Coastal waters off of every continent except Antarctica.
- Like many other sharks, females are larger than males.

OCEANIC WHITETIP SHARK

I'm an **oceanic whitetip shark.** I get a bad rep for being aggressive, but I'm really not so scary. I live a pretty tough life as a solitary swimmer who slowly roams the open ocean. It can be tough out there in the middle of nowhere, and food can be difficult to find. Some people refer to the open ocean as the blue desert! But if you give me a chance, you'll see I'm not so bad. Some fish even depend on me! Remoras are fish that have special suckers that allow them to attach to my body. I give them a ride across the ocean, and they earn their keep by eating parasites off me. I'm even pretty photogenic, if I do say so myself. So, please be nice to oceanic whitetip sharks!

NURSE SHARK

I'm a **nurse shark**. You may have noticed that most of my sharky friends enjoy swimming around. But swimming isn't really my thing. Sure, I can do it, but unlike many sharks, I spend a lot of my time just relaxing on the sand. Even though we live underwater, sharks still need to breathe. We do that through little openings in our bodies called gills that help us get oxygen from water. Most sharks find it easiest to get oxygen by swimming. But I've got super-strong muscles that help me pump water through my gills without moving around that much. Remember that the next time you're being a couch potato—you and I are not that different. So, please be nice to nurse sharks!

CARIBBEAN REEF SHARK

Nice to meet you! I'm a **Caribbean reef shark**. Unlike a lot of my shark friends, I live near coral reefs. You know those really beautiful, colorful underwater worlds, right? Not to brag, but some people consider me to be the guardian of the reef because I am vital to their survival. You see, coral reefs are fragile, and I help protect them. My job, as the top predator, is to make sure the food chain is in balance. If I weren't around, there would be too many of the fish I like to eat, and then they would eat up all the smaller fish. Without me, those reefs wouldn't be nearly as neat. Save the reef! Save the Caribbean reef shark! Be nice to us both!

CARIBBEAN REEF SHARK FACTS

- **Weight:** Up to 154 pounds (70 kilograms).
- **Length:** Up to 10 feet (3 meters).
- **Diet:** Small fish, squid, octopus, and some rays.
- Caribbean reef sharks are active more at night than during the day.
- Caribbean reef sharks give birth to live young, not eggs.
- They are one of the most common and well-studied sharks in the Caribbean.

WOBBEGONG SHARK

Oh, hello up there! How're you doing? I'm a wobbegong shark. You might be wondering why I look so funny. Yes, I know—I look more like a weedy rock than a shark, but there's a method to my madness. The reason I'm so crazy looking is because I spend much of my time lying on the ocean floor. Lucky me, right? My flat shape and wild colors help camouflage me so nobody will bother me. It also helps me catch prey because they don't realize I'm hiding out nearby. It's like hide-and-seek! Pretty neat, huh? So, please be nice to wobbegong sharks!

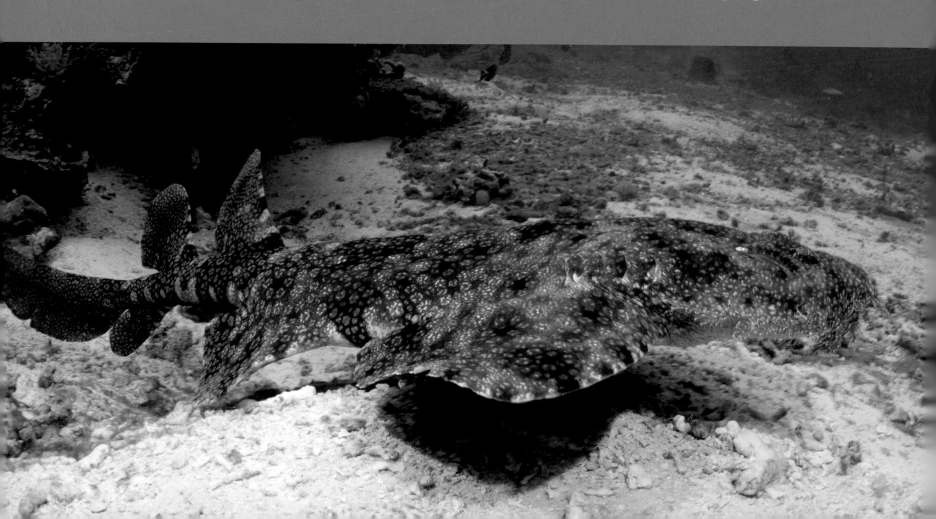

BROADNOSE SEVENGILL SHARK

'Sup? I'm a **broadnose sevengill shark**. I'm part of a group of sharks known as cow sharks (don't ask me why!), and we're the oldest sharks in the world. In fact, cow sharks have been around for over 190 million years. That's way older than you humans. We were around at the same time as the dinosaurs! Respect your elders, and please be nice to broadnose sevengill sharks!

LEMON SHARK

I'm a **lemon shark**. I get my name because in the right light I look yellowish, like a lemon. Another thing you may notice is my teeth! I've got up to five rows of these bad boys! If one of my teeth falls out, no problemo! I can just replace it with a tooth from the row behind it. When I was young, I would lose every single one of my teeth one at a time every seven or eight days. Think about how busy the lemon shark tooth fairy must be! And next time you're swimming in the Caribbean, take a look at the sandy ocean floor. You might just find one of my old teeth. So, please be nice to lemon sharks!

LEMON SHARK FACTS

- **Length:** Up to 11 feet (3.5 meters) long.
- **Weight:** Up 405 pounds (180 kilograms).
- Lemon sharks are bottom dwellers, and they often find prey by searching in the sand.
- Their curved teeth help them catch slippery fish.
- The yellowish color of lemon sharks is believed to help them camouflage with the sand below them.
- They are social sharks, and often as many as twenty lemon sharks will group together.

BULL SHARK

I'm a **bull shark**. You can find me pretty much anywhere there's water. That includes both oceans and rivers! Yup—the coolest thing about me is that I'm able to live in both saltwater and freshwater. For most sharks, going from the ocean to a river would be a lot like one of you humans trying to go to outer space without a spacesuit on, but I have special adaptations that allow me to be equally at home in either type of water. Wouldn't it be nice if you could go from Earth to space that easily? Scientists believe humans can learn a lot from bull sharks' unique adaptations, so please be nice to us!

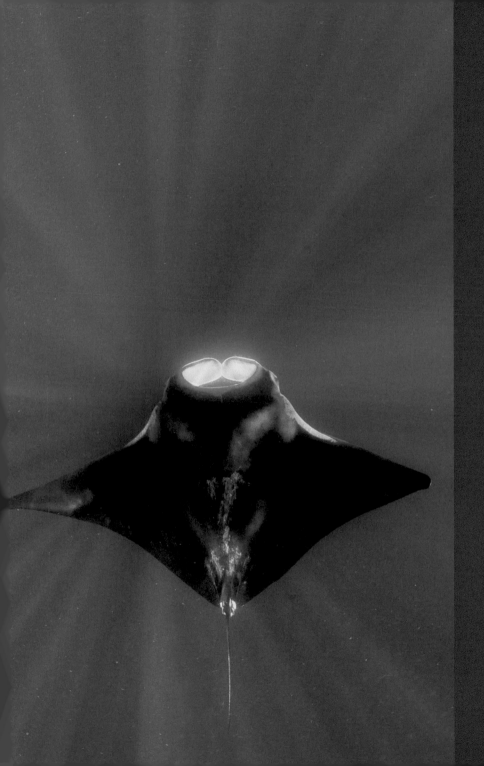

MANTA RAY

Hey, I'm a **manta ray**. You're probably thinking, "What is this ray doing in a book about sharks?" Well, let me tell you—manta rays and all these sharks you met earlier are closely related. We're like cousins. But just like sharks, we're being overfished, and there are not many of us left. My gill plates, which are used to catch the tiny plankton I eat, are prized in China. So, some fishermen are catching us just for that one specific body part. But even when I'm not being targeted, I'm often accidentally caught by fishing boats trying to catch other fish. These boat use really long nets, sometimes miles long, that are hard for us to see, so we get tangled up in them. Every year thousands of manta rays are accidently caught for no reason and discarded back into the ocean. This is called by-catch, and it's a big reason our populations are decreasing. So I just wanted to sneak in here and say we're cool too, so please be nice to manta rays!

HOW TO BE NICE TO SHARKS

There are some simple things you can do to help sharks. First, it's never a good idea to hunt sharks or eat shark fin soup. Shark fin soup is a flavorless soup that has shark fins for an ingredient. It's possible that 73 million sharks a year are killed for their fins to meet the demand for shark fin soup. So the most important way to be nice to sharks is pretty easy—just don't eat them! And if you're really nice, only eat seafood caught in responsible ways. Big fishing fleets will often use a long line with thousands of baited hooks on it to catch fish. These hooks accidentally catch sharks—and many other ocean animals! If you avoid eating the seafood caught this way, you'll be helping out the sharks too.

Even though sharks don't want to eat humans, they do have lots of teeth and sometimes make mistakes. Sharks like to eat seals, and sometimes people swimming on the surface of ocean, especially on surfboards, look like seals. Sharks don't hunt humans on purpose.

Many shark species have been overfished, which means there are a lot fewer of them now than there used to be. So, please be nice to all the sharks in the sea, not just the ones listed in this book. Without sharks, ocean life would collapse. And without a healthy ocean, lots of people would suffer. So, besides being nice to sharks because it's the cool thing to do, it's also really important for us humans as well. The best part is that being nice to sharks is easy. It's important to let your friends, family, and teachers know that sharks aren't the vicious monsters people think—they are much more beneficial to humans alive than dead.

ABOUT THE AUTHOR

Matt Weiss is an award-winning photographer, journalist, dive expedition organizer, and filmmaker. Matt's favorite shark is the biggest one of all, the whale shark, but he also loves all the small critters that live in the ocean too. Matt has contributed to many international publications, including *Sport Diving Magazine*, *National Geographic*, and *Asian Geographic*. He is constantly searching for new ocean animals to photograph and spends lots of time on the bottom of the sea looking for small fish and crustaceans. His favorite place to dive is Antarctica, but when he's not swimming with sharks, he's the publisher of DivePhotoGuide.com, the world's largest underwater photography publication. *Please Be Nice to Sharks* is his first book. Matt lives in Brooklyn, New York.

INDEX